Great Ideas

Program Authors

Connie Juel, Ph.D.

Jeanne R. Paratore, Ed.D.

Deborah Simmons, Ph.D.

Sharon Vaughn, Ph.D.

PEARSON

Scott Foresman

Glenview, Illinois
Boston, Massachusetts
Chandler, Arizona
Upper Saddle River, New Jersey

ISBN-13: 978-0-328-45273-6
ISBN-10: 0-328-45273-4

10 V011 14

Great Ideas

Clever Solutions

IDEAS
That Change Our World

Contents

4

Think Smart

See page 29 for My New Words!

Think Smart

A cat is up in a tall tree! Kids want that cat down. What can kids do? Kids can think smart!

Kids can get a long stick and ribbon. Then they can shake the stick and ribbon. Cats like to chase ribbon. That cat will get down.

This girl has a big mess in her desk. She puts things away. The mess gets taller and taller. Things get harder to find. What can she do?

She can place her things in a small box. Yes! That's all it took. Kids can think smart!

One kid can lift a big box. Two kids can lift a bigger box. But they can't lift the biggest box. What can these kids do?

They can ask for help. A bunch of
kids together can lift the biggest box!
That's it! Kids can think smart!

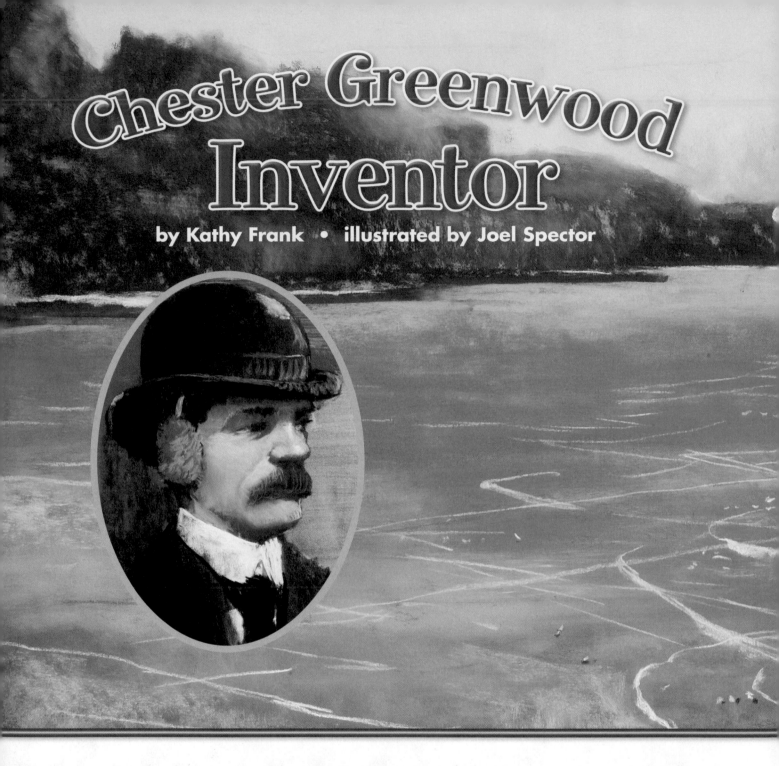

Chester Greenwood Inventor

by Kathy Frank • illustrated by Joel Spector

Chester put on his hat and scarf. He got his ice skates and went to the pond. "This scarf makes my ears itch," he said. "I can't skate when my ears itch."

Chester took off his scarf and
went home. What could he find to
fix his problem?

At home, Chester got wire and bent it. He added fur at the ends. Then Chester put that wire and fur on his ears. His ears felt warm!

Chester went back to the pond.
He put on his skates and went to the
edge. These muffs kept his ears warm.

Chester went faster and faster on
the ice. These wire and fur muffs kept
his ears warm for a long time.

"Where did you get those?"
pals asked.

"I made them," said Chester.

"These are muffs for my ears."

Chester made muffs for all his pals. Then he added a bigger band and thicker fur. People far away asked for these muffs. We all still use them!

Did those kids back then think that Chester was smart? Yes, they did. What do you think? Did Chester think smart? You can be the judge!

The Bus Pass

by Marjorie Fitzmann • illustrated by Liz Conrad

Madge and her mom sat at the bus stop. Madge held on to her bus pass. Wind swirled. Madge grabbed her hat. Her bus pass drifted away.

Her pass landed in back of a hedge.
Madge stuck her hand far into that
hedge. But she didn't get her pass.

Madge picked up a long stick at the edge of the grass. She stuck it into the hedge. But it did not get close. "I will find a longer stick," she said.

Madge got a longer stick and stuck it in the hedge. She got close, but she still didn't pick up her pass.

"I need gum," Madge said.

"Gum?" Mom asked.

"Yes, Mom," Madge nodded.

"I think gum will help."

The gum was sticky. Madge took it and put it on the stick. She stuck the stick into the hedge.

Her bus pass stuck to the gum.
"I got my pass!" yelled Madge.
Mom grinned and said, "Madge,
that was smart!"

Just then, the bus stopped. "I saw that!" said the man on the bus. "You are the smartest girl I've seen!"

"Thanks!" said Madge with the biggest grin ever.

Riddle Time

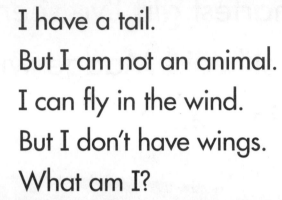

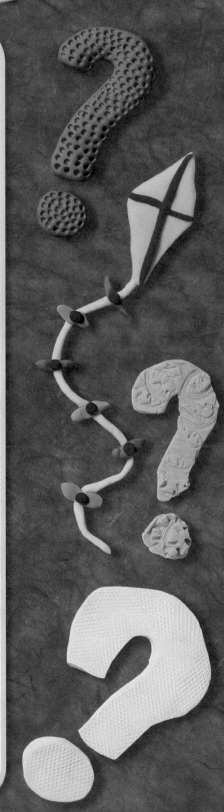

I have a tail.
But I am not an animal.
I can fly in the wind.
But I don't have wings.
What am I?

I have a face.
But I cannot smile.
I have hands.
But I don't have fingers.
What am I?

I have legs.
But I cannot walk.
I have arms.
But I have no hands.
What am I?

Answers: a kite, a clock, a chair

My New Words

away*   Stay **away** from the street.

find*   When you **find** something, you look for it and get it.

hedge   A **hedge** is a thick row of bushes or small trees planted as a fence.

long*   If something is **long**, there is a lot of space from the beginning to the end of it.

took*   Who **took** my book?

warm   If something is **warm**, it is more hot than cold.

*tested high-frequency words

Contents

New Ideas

See page 53 for My New Words!

New Ideas

It's a rainy day. Rain, rain, rain!
Kids can stay in and not get wet.
But kids can still have fun when it
rains. Kids can paint. Kids can write.

Kids can sit on a rug with a big book. Can two kids see the same book at the same time? Yes! Kids can sit side by side. This way is fun.

Most kids don't like to play games out in the rain. But kids can still play. These pals play. Five pals play with one ball. Pals can take turns!

When it rains, kids still have fun!
Kids can play. Kids can play with pals.
Kids won't say, "Rain, rain, go away!"
Kids will say, "We like rainy days!"

Rainy Day Fun!
• Play games
• Share books
• Paint
• Write stories

Rosa Parks

by Colin Timms

Rosa Parks worked hard all day. Then she went and waited for a bus to take her home.

A bus stopped. Rosa got on and sat down. After more stops, the bus was filled.

In 1955 some buses had rules.

Black people and white people could not sit together. And if a bus was filled, black people had to let white people sit first.

A white man got on Rosa's bus. The man that drove this bus said Rosa must let the man sit in her seat.

"I won't leave this seat," she said.

Rosa Parks did a brave thing. She just sat still. She stayed in her seat. She broke the rule. For this, Rosa Parks was sent to jail.

People got mad and yelled, "Don't ride buses! These are bad rules!"

For more than a year, most black people did not ride buses. They walked or rode in cars.

Rosa Parks helped people see that the bus rule was bad. It was time to write a rule that treated all people on buses the same.

Rosa Parks spoke up and helped us see things in new ways. Today black people and white people ride together. We can thank Rosa Parks for that.

What a Meal!

by Gabriel Robin

illustrated by Luciana Navarro Powell

A man with a pack on his back walked up to Miss Gail and spoke, "I have walked a long way and need rest. May I stay and eat here?"

"Keep walking," Miss Gail snapped as she hung a pot with water on the fire. Miss Gail was grumpy and mean. "We don't have much, and it won't feed us all."

"But I have all that we need," said
the man. He got a stone from his pack
and held it up. "Most people can't make
meals from stone," he said. "But I can."

"A meal from this small stone?" asked Miss Gail. "Let's see that!"

The man dropped the stone in the big pot and stirred it.

"Do we have turnips?" the man asked. "This stone and turnips will make a nice meal."

Miss Gail added turnips to the pot.

"Last time, I had a nice meal with meat in this pot," the man said. "We have meat!" Ray called. He got it. Then he dropped it in the pot.

"A meal with grain is nice," said Lee.
"We can get rice!" called Dean.
Then Miss Gail took a sip. "Yum!"
she said. "All we needed was the stone!"

"Can we write how to make this?"
asked Ray. "May we keep the stone?"

"I must keep it," said the man. "I
may need it for my next meal."

Make a Taco

What can you do with meat, lettuce, beans, and cheese? You can make a taco.

Here's what you will need.

- cooked taco meat or beans
- taco shells
- shredded lettuce
- chopped tomato
- salsa
- shredded cheddar cheese

1. Get a taco shell.

2. Put some meat or beans into the shell.

3. Add lettuce, tomato, salsa, and cheese.

Enjoy your taco!

My New Words

don't*   **Don't** is a short way to write *do not*.
                 Don't be late for dinner.

most*   **Most** people like music.

turnips   **Turnips** are vegetables that grow underground like carrots.

won't*   **Won't** is a short way to write *will not*.
                 I **won't** be able to help you.

write*   When you **write**, you make letters or words.

*tested high-frequency words

Contents

Finding Answers

See page 81 for My New Words!

Finding Answers

Kids get to pick a class pet. Kids want to get a ferret. But would a ferret make a good class pet? Kids can check it out.

Kids can ask. What is a ferret? What should these pets eat? Will these pets play well with kids? Will they sleep much?

Where can kids get facts? Kids can try this first. Start with this small box. Print *ferrets* in this small box. Then push this button.

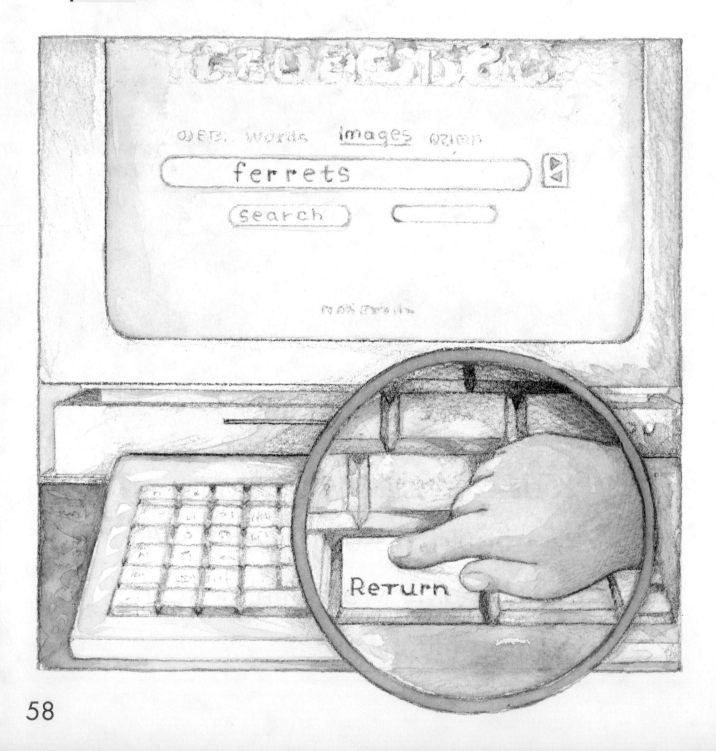

Kids can read what ferrets eat.
These pets eat the same things that
kittens eat. Ferrets like kittens' snacks.
Yum! Yum! Yum!

Kids can get facts by reading
books. Pick books and take a close
look. Can kids play with ferrets? Yes.
Kids will like playing with ferrets.

Ferrets play in tunnels. Bags can be a ferret's tunnels. These pets play with small balls too.

Kids can get facts by talking to people. This is a vet's place. Vets can tell us about pets. Do ferrets sleep a lot? Kids can ask vets.

Yes. Ferrets like to sleep a lot. Some ferrets may like to sleep with a rag over them. But ferrets like to eat and play with kids too.

Is a pet ferret lots of hard work? Is it fun? Would it be a good class pet?

Kids can ask. Kids can get facts.
Kids can pick a class pet!

Plants Drink Water

by Julian Henry

Plants need water to grow big and tall. Can plants drink water? Yes! And you can show it. Just get white mums, vases, red drops, and water.

First, fill vases partway with water. Next, put ten red drops in each vase. The water should turn red. If it's not dark, add ten more drops.

Next, let a grown-up cut the bottom off each stem. Then put one white mum in each vase.

Leave the mums in the vases. Let them soak for more than a day. Then check them over to see what happens.

First, the stems turn red. Up and up, dark red water pushes up the stems. Then each plant's blossoms turn red.

Water flows up the stems and to the blossoms. Did you know this would happen? This is the way plants drink water and grow!

Find the Seeds

by Kathleen Franz

illustrated by Laura Merer

At lunch Coach had eggs and a peach. Willow had ham and a plum. Sloan had fish and peas and a big, red strawberry.

Coach leaned over his tray and
bit his peach. He showed Willow and
Sloan the pit. "This is the peach's seed.
Find the seeds in your lunch," he said.

Willow held up her plum and bit it.
She showed the pit. "This is the plum's
seed," she said.

Sloan pushed his fish to the side.
He picked up his big, red strawberry
and bit into it. He did not find a
seed inside.

"There is one big seed in Coach's peach. There is one big seed in Willow's plum. There should be a seed in my strawberry!" Sloan said.

"Would you look again?" asked Coach. "I think you'll see seeds." "I can't see seeds in Sloan's strawberry," said Willow.

"That's it!" called Sloan.
"What?" asked Willow.
Sloan grinned. "Seeds are not **inside** my strawberry. They are **outside**!"

"We spotted all the seeds, Coach!" called Willow.

Coach had a smile. Lunch was fun that day!

Why Do You Ask?

1 Why would you want to know what the weather is like?

2 Why would you want to know about dinosaurs?

3 Why would you want to know about life on a farm or in a city?

4 Why would you want to know how your body works?

5 Why would you want to know what the moon is made of?

My New Words

blossoms   **Blossoms** are flowers.

ferret   A **ferret** is a small furry animal.

over*   They came **over** to our house after school.
The dog jumped **over** the stick.

push*   When you **push** something, you move it away from you.

should*   You **should** eat breakfast every day.

would*   **Would** you like an apple?
They said they **would** wait for us.

*tested high-frequency words

Contents

Take-It-Easy IDEAS

See page 109 for My New Words!

Take-It-Easy Ideas

We have small pages with stories. We need one big page. We can set two pages side by side. Soon we will have one big page of stories.

How will these pages stay together? Can we clip them? Yes! But clips may not stay. Wait! Can we use tape? Yes! Tape helps with this job!

Lots of kids love grape drink. But grape drink is hard to take in the car. It spills and stains the seats. Moms and dads don't like spills.

Wait! Can we use drink boxes? Yes! It is much better to sip grape drink from a box! Then moms and dads will be happier.

It is hard to get all this stuff up these steps. It is too much for one trip. It falls and scatters behind you.

Wait! Let's place these supplies in a backpack. Pull the backpack up on your back. Yes! That is much better!

A Cool Cast

by Hector Perez • illustrated by Carol Newsom

Krysta Morlan hadn't walked well from the time she was a small girl. Then her doctor treated her leg. He put on a cast to help her leg heal.

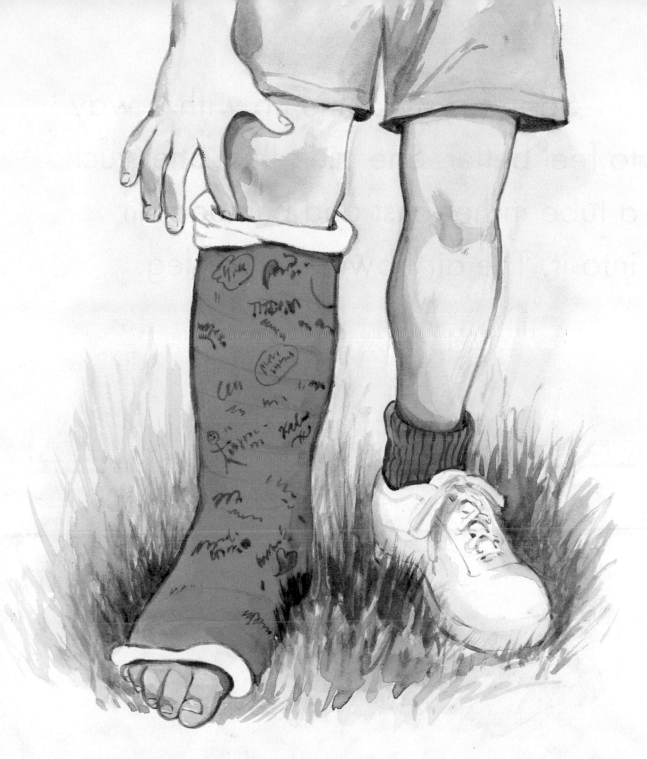

On hot days, Krysta's skin itched inside her hard cast. Krysta wished she could scratch it. She wanted to pull off her cast, but she could not.

Soon Krysta came up with a way to feel better. She tried this. She stuck a tube in her cast and pumped air into it. The air flowed on her leg.

At last Krysta felt better! The air made the itch stop. Krysta kept the pump strapped snug on her leg. This gadget made Krysta much happier.

Inventor's Contest

Now Krysta did not need to
scratch, scratch, scratch! She wanted
to share her gadget. She showed it at
a contest.

Girl Wins Contest With Smart Gadget

People cried, "Who is behind this?" It was Krysta! Her gadget was the best in this contest! This teen had made a gadget people could love.

Krysta planned more things that help. She made a bike that floats on water. Splish! Splash! Kids who did not walk well had fun with this bike.

What will Krysta think of next?
We will just have to wait and see!

A Ramp for Stripes

by Joy Williams

illustrated by Pete Whitehead

Brad went with his mom and dad to get a puppy. Brad spied three puppies. One was black, one was spotted, and one had stripes.

"Brad, I don't think you need to pick a puppy," said Mom. "Look at that puppy walking behind you. That puppy picked you!"

At home, Brad played with the puppy and petted it all day long. Stroke, stroke, stroke. Soon the puppy slept in Brad's lap.

"Let's call him Stripes," Brad said. Brad picked up Stripes and set him on the window seat. Stripes wagged his tail and went back to sleep.

Each day, Brad and Stripes
played and played. When Stripes got
sleepy, he sat down by the window
and wagged his tail.

"Look, Mom and Dad!" called Brad.
"Stripes loves that window seat!"
"He would like to nap in the sun,"
Dad added.

Stripes stayed at the window and wagged his tail.

"Stripes can't pull himself up on the seat," cried Brad. "He's too small!"

"What can we do?" asked Dad.
"Let's make a ramp," called Brad.
"That's a fine plan. Stripes will be
happier if he can get up," said Mom.

Dad, Mom, and Brad all worked
together to make the ramp. Soon they
had the perfect ramp for Stripes.

"Step up, Stripes," Brad called.

Stripes stepped on the ramp and hurried to the top. He peeked out the window and wagged his tail. Then Stripes curled up to nap in the sun.

Did You Know?

- An inventor saw burrs caught in his dog's fur. That gave him an idea for a new kind of fastener.

- The first elevator was called "The Flying Chair."

- The first computers were about as big as refrigerators.

My New Words

behind* Who is **behind** me? Her class is **behind** in its work.

doctor A **doctor** is a person who helps people stay healthy.

gadget A **gadget** is a small tool that helps with a task.

love* **Love** is a warm, good feeling you have for someone or something. She feels **love** for her puppy.

pull* When you **pull** something, you move it toward you.

soon* **Soon** means in a short time.

Contents

Then and Now Ideas

See page 135 for My New Words!

Then and Now Ideas

Before we had cars and planes,
we rode horses. We rode in buggies.
It was not fast.

112

Now we can go faster in cars. Now we can fly in planes. A plane flies high in the sky. Planes fly very fast.

We can send letters to tell things.
But it might take days to get letters.
Now we can send e-mail. It's
fast. You can be sure this is quick.

We can use phones to tell things too. First we had phones at home. Then we had pay phones for calls outside. Now we have cell phones.

Phones at home

Pay phone

Cell phone

At first people played games like this. None of these games had lights. None made beeps and buzzes.

But now we can play a new kind of game. These games have bright lights! They bing and buzz! These games zap and flash!

Scrub! Scrub!

by Virginia Wozniak

In the past, people washed things
in streams. Some still do. It is hard
work to make sure things get clean.

Dip! Scrub!

Dip! Scrub! Dip! Scrub! This kind of washing is hard to do. Then people hung things outside to dry.

Later people washed things at home. They made bubbles with soap. They scrubbed in the sink. None of this was simple.

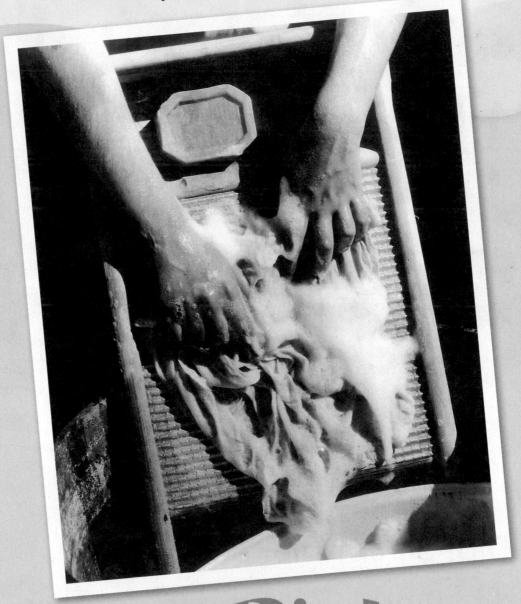

Dip!
Scrub!

Dip! Scrub! Dip! Scrub! Dip! Scrub! People hung things on outside lines. It took lots of time to wash and dry like this.

Jiggle!

Fill the tub. Add soap. Drop shirts in. Plop! Plop! Plop! Jiggle! Wiggle! Jiggle! Wiggle! Squeeze shirts.

Drip! Drip! This way takes a little less time. Shirts get clean and bright. But people still dried shirts outside.

Plop!

Now people can use these to wash and dry things. Plop! Plop! Plop! Just drop shirts and pants in. Add soap. That's it!

Tumble!

Then put things in here to dry.
Tumble! Tumble! It dries things fast.
This way is not hard at all. Before
long, all is clean.

Popple Popcorn

by Denise Plainfield
illustrated by Liz Goulet Dubois

This is Pete Popple. He makes popcorn and sells it. Kids like his popcorn. Moms and dads like his popcorn. Here's how it all started.

Last spring, Pete went to a
ballgame. Before he went, he made
popcorn. Pete did not want dull
popcorn. He added lots of spices.

Mom said, "This sure tastes yummy.
It tastes a little like apple pie."
Pete filled a big bag with popcorn.
Then Pete left for the game.

At the game, Pete gave popcorn to his buddies.

"Yum! Yum!" they said. "We like this kind of popcorn!"

The next day, Pete made more.

"It's sweet," said Calvin.

"It's very light," said Ty.

"It tastes like apple pie," said Gail.

"How did you make it?" asked Ty's mom.

"It's simple," said Pete. "I just popped popcorn and added spices."

That day people ate lots of popcorn. Before long, none was left! "You should sell this popcorn," said his buddies.

And that's what Pete did. He made lots of popcorn. At each game, people yelled, "Popple Popcorn is best! Keep popping, Pete!"

Popple Popcorn

Airplane Art

by Kimberly M. Hutmacher

Zigging, zagging
Way up high
Painting pictures
in the sky!

Something to Think About

by Carolyn Forsyth

When airplanes get as thick as cars,
And people ride from Earth to Mars,
Will traffic lights be made of stars?

My New Words

before*   Please clean your room **before** you play.

kind*   A **kind** is a group of things that are alike in some way.

none*   **None** of these books are mine.

phones   **Phones** are used to talk to people far away.

spice   Pepper is a **spice.** Ginger is too.

sure*   Are you **sure** you locked the door?

wash   To **wash** something means to clean it with soap and water.

*tested high-frequency words

Contents

A New Use

See page 159 for My New Words!

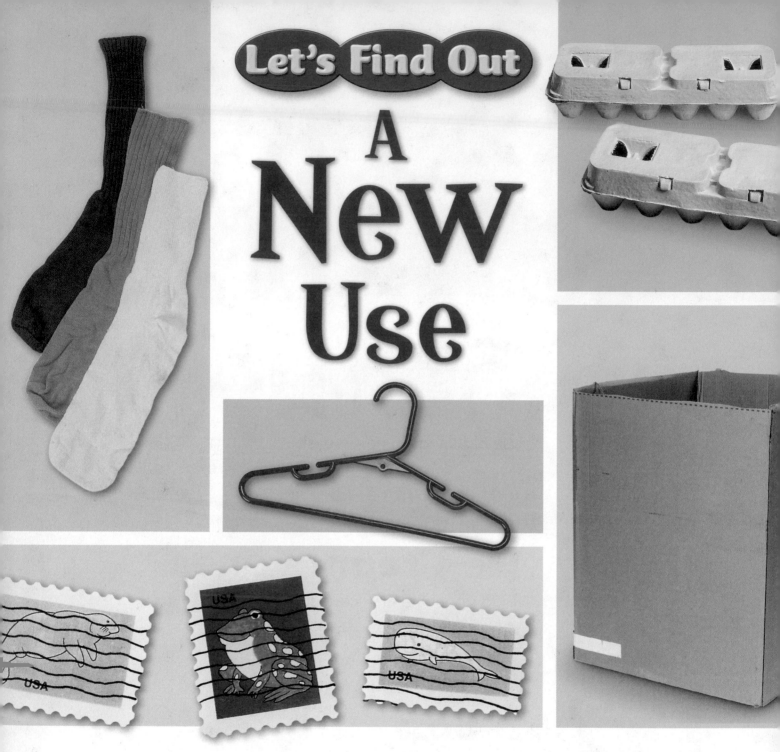

A New Use

Using things in new ways can be fun. We can look for things where we live or at school. How can we use these things in new ways?

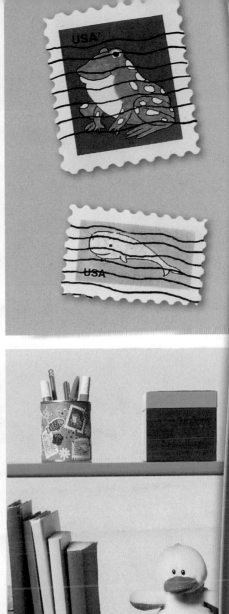

This cute can with pasted stamps can be used for pens. It goes well on a desk or shelf.

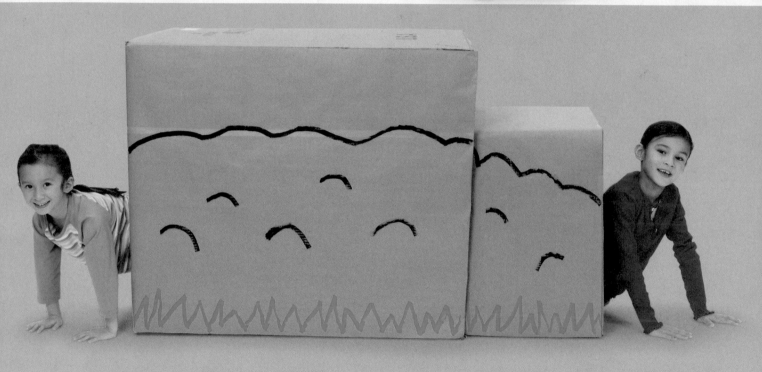

Boxes can be fun because we can do lots with them. Make a cave. Poking in and out is fun! Boxes can be used for lots of games.

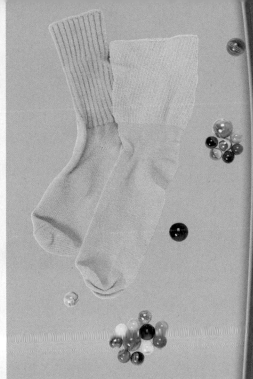
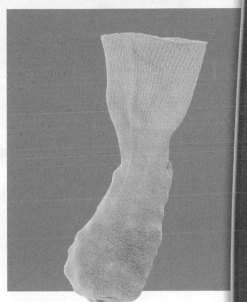

Socks can be used in new ways. Keep marbles in big socks. Plink! Plank! Plunk! Keep pennies in a small sock. Clink! Clank! Clunk!

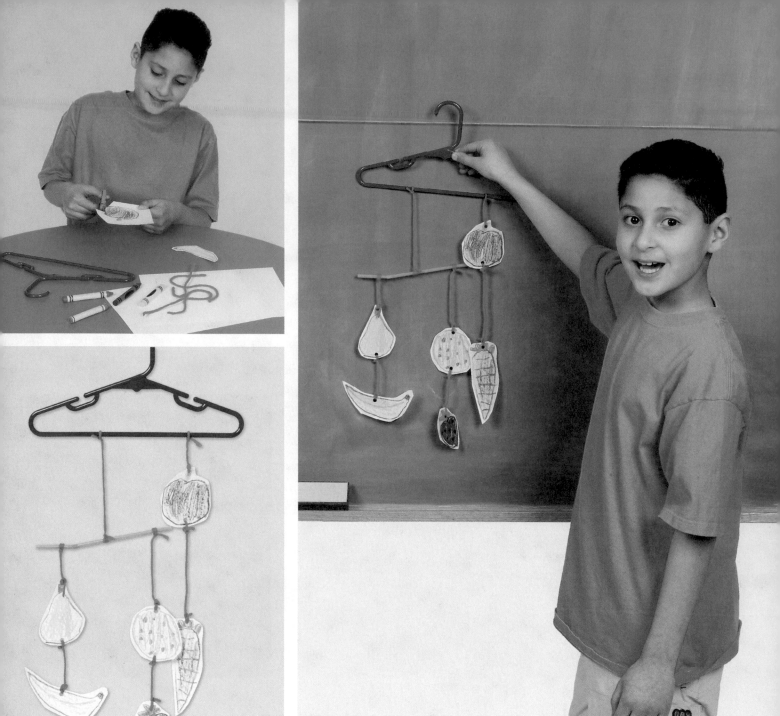

We can make things at school.
We cut shapes and punch holes in
them. We tie strings to the shapes.
Then we tie the shapes to hangers.

If we sort these odds and ends, making things will go quicker. We can pick up what we need fast.

What can you use in new ways?

Ice-Cream Cones

by Nancy Haley

Ice cream is yummy! We can eat
ice cream in cups. We can eat it in
dishes. And we can eat it in cones.
Cones? How did we get cones?

In 1904, lots of people visited a big fair. Kids went because school had ended. Everyone had fun and ate yummy treats.

It was a hot summer. Frozen treats were just what everyone needed.

A man was selling ice cream. He served it in dishes.

Soon this man used up all his dishes! But he still had lots of ice cream left.

This ice-cream man was working near a man making waffles. The waffle man was clever. He curled a waffle into a cone shape.

He and the ice-cream man put ice cream inside this waffle cone. At that moment, the ice-cream cone was invented!

Ice-cream cones were a big hit.
No one needed cups or dishes!
People had to lick fast because ice
cream melts and drips.

When an ice-cream truck goes by where you live, think of that clever waffle man at the fair. He used waffles in a crazy but super way.

More Than Just a Box

by Lynn Cooper
illustrated by Page O'Rourke

At school Miss Naple saved boxes.
She had little boxes and big boxes.
"Let's use these boxes in clever
new ways," said Miss Naple.

Josh began by using tops of boxes
for framing his pictures. First, he
taped pictures on the backs of the
frames. Then he added tiny stars.

Ned made a secret place for his critters to live. He painted a box. Next, he set his critters inside. Then he placed his box on the table.

Jill put stones in her box. She
closed the box and taped the lid.
She used bright yarn. Her cat will
like chasing this box.

Patty had five boxes for a train.
She taped on wheels. Next, she tied
string to the boxes.

"My train goes fast!" joked Patty.

Josh, Patty, Jill, and Ned smiled
because they were smart. They had
used boxes in new ways! It was easy.
You can try it too.

 # Buttons!

Read Together

Shirts have buttons. Coats have buttons. Buttons come in all colors. Some buttons are big. Some are small.

Make a picture. You will need paper, a pencil, glue, and buttons.

1. Draw a picture on paper.
2. Add glue to one side of a button.
3. Stick the button onto the picture.
4. Add more buttons.

You have made a button picture!

158

My New Words

because*
She cried **because** she broke her leg.

fair
A **fair** is an outdoor show with rides, food, and other events.

goes*
My little sister **goes** where I go.

live*
When you **live**, you breathe and grow. Your home is where you **live**.

school*
A **school** is a place where you learn things.

waffle
A **waffle** is a flat cake with square dents on both sides.

*tested high-frequency words

Acknowledgments

Text

Every effort has been made to locate the copyright owner of material reproduced in this component. Omissions brought to our attention will be corrected in subsequent editions. Grateful acknowledgment is made to the following for copyrighted material.

134 Kimberly M. Hutmacher "Airplane Art" by Kimberly M. Hutmacher from *www.atozkidstuff.com/tran.html*. Used by permission of the author.

134 Carolyn Forsyth "Something to Think About" by Carolyn Forsyth from *Jack and Jill Magazine.*

Illustrations

Cover: Brenda Sexton, Alan Flinn, Page O'Rourke
2, 55, 80 Brenda Sexton; 2, 31, 52 Simon Shaw; 4, 20–27 Liz Conrad; 5–11 Holli Conger; 12–18 Joel Spector; 30, 44–51 Luciana Navarro Powell; 32–35 Bob McMahon; 54, 72–79 Laura Merer; 56–65 John Wallner; 82–83, 98–107 Pete Whitehead; 90–97 Carol Newsom; 108, 160 Mike Gibbie; 110, 126–133 Liz Goulet Dubois; 111, 134 Alan Flinn; 136, 152–157 Page O'Rourke; 136, 147–148 Stephen Snider.

Photographs

Every effort has been made to secure permission and provide appropriate credit for photographic material. The publisher deeply regrets any omission and pledges to correct errors called to its attention in subsequent editions.

Unless otherwise acknowledged, all photographs are the property of Pearson Education, Inc.

Photo locators denoted as follows: Top (T), Center (C), Bottom (B), Left (L), Right (R), Background (Bkgd)

3 (BR) ©Retofile/Getty Images; 31 (CR) ©Don Cravens/Time & Life Pictures/Getty Images; 36 (C) ©Time Life Pictures/Getty Images; 37 (C) ©Time & Life Pictures/Getty Images; 38 (C) Getty Images; 39 (C) ©Time & Life Pictures/Getty Images; 40 (C) ©AP/Wide World Photos; 41 (C) ©Time & Life Pictures/Getty Images; 42 (C) ©Don Cravens/Time & Life Pictures/Getty Images; 43 (C) ©Bettmann/Corbis; 111 (CR) Getty Images; 112 (C) Getty Images, (C) ©Time Life Pictures/Getty Images; 113 (CC) ©Royalty-Free/Corbis, (C) Getty Images; 114 (TR, CL, BR, BC) Getty Images, (CL) ©Retrofile/Getty Images; 115 (BL) ©fStop/Getty Images, (TR) Getty Images, (TL) ©Retofile/Getty Images, (BR) Stockdisc; 116 (C) Getty Images, (CC) ©Retrofile/Getty Images; 117 (C) Getty Images; 118 (C) Getty Images; 119 (C) Getty Images; 120 (C) Getty Images; 121 (C) Getty Images; 122 (C) ©Schenectady Museum/Hall of Electrical History Foundation/Corbis; 123 (C) Getty Images; 124 (C) ©Brownie Harris/Corbis; 137 (CR) Getty Images; 144 (TR, TL, C) Getty Images, (C) Jupiter Images; 145 (C) Getty Images; 146 (C) Corbis, (CR) Getty Images; 149 (TR, TL, C) Getty Images; 150 (L) Getty Images, (C) Montague Lyon Collection/Missouri Historical Society, (TL) Stockdisc; 151 (CR) ©Image Source/Getty Images, (TC) ©Stephen Mallon/Getty Images.